To wis … st
in your further research
into women's realities.
Your fond friend,
Mary

The Better Half

Women's Voices

The Better Half

Women's Voices

a collection of poetic monologues
inspired by women's diaries

By Betty Jane Wylie

BMP
Black Moss Press

Published by Black Moss Press
2450 Byng Road, Windsor, Ontario, N8W 3E8.
Black Moss Press books are distributed in Canada
and the United States by Firefly Books Ltd.,
250 Sparks Ave., Willowdale, Ontario, M2H 2S4.
All orders should be directed there.

Financial assistance toward publication of this book was
provided by the Canada Council, the Department of Canadian Heritage
and the Ontario Arts Council.

Cover design by Richard Withey
Layout and page design by Kristina Carroll.

Canadian Cataloguing in Publication Data:
The better half : women's voices : a collection of women's voices
inspired by their diaries and poetic monlogues
Poems.
ISBN 0-88753-280-2
1. Wylie, Betty Jane, 1931—
Ps8283.W6B48 1995 811'.54089287 C95-9006505-6
PR9195.3.B48 1995

To Janice, Meg, Jennifer, Paige and Emily
in the hope that one of you will keep a diary

ACKNOWLEDGEMENTS

My thanks to the Canada Council; a short-term grant enabled me to finish this project. I am also grateful to Don Coles, Kathy Fretwell and Richard Teleky for their criticism and advice, and of course, to Marty Gervais. This is my sixth book for Black Moss Press, and I thank him for his faith in me.

CONTENTS

Introduction: "Be Nice"

Women at last have found a voice.
In other times they had no choice
    But to obey—
And don't forget—to honour, love
(Whatever were we thinking of?),
    Work night and day.

Daily duties of home and sink
Kept most too occupied to think
    About rebellion.
The odd one who escaped the yoke
Ended up alone and broke,
    Branded a hellion.

In other ages they were burnt,
And so most women quickly learnt
    To toe the line.
Silence was golden, and safer too,
To follow without much ado
    The grand design.

He for God alone, and she
For God in him, and she must see
    That it is right:
Hers the hearth and his the field
His to rule and hers to yield
    To his birthright.

She memorized the ritual
And it became habitual—
    A daily nostrum—
A few apt words to keep the peace,
Lines repeated without cease
    From holy rostrum.

We've all been taught what to expect
If we're unwilling to protect
    The family jewels.
In our submission lies our strength,
So all of us have learned at length
    These rigid rules:

OLD RULES

Thou shalt remember to be nice,
Bearing in mind the good advice
    Of grandmother:
You catch more flies with honey than
With vinegar (for every man
    Wants his mother).

Thou shalt love, honor and obey,
Not only on your wedding day,
    But all your life.
No one gave you any choice;
You're expected to rejoice
    To be a wife.

Thou shalt always shut your eyes
To nasty facts and compromise
    Your deepest feeling,
Always smiling through your tears
Never letting on your fears—
    They're too revealing.

Above all, don't complain, keep smiling.
Most men consider that beguiling—
    Not soggy tears.
So dry your eyes and shut them tight
And when you spread your legs at night
    Remember, dears,

Don't talk, don't think, bear up, bear down.
Be good, be patient, never frown,
    But don't be awed.
He doesn't, as yet, wear a crown.
Remember, husband is a noun;
    He is not God.

But women kept on trying to think,
And so they turned to pen and ink
    To write their lives.
Lifewriting's what we call it now,
A form of lit, though not highbrow,
    Written by wives.

Singles, too, young girls whose names
Would be forgot but for their aims
    To validate
Their lives—just facts, not true confessions.
Someone might read their indiscretions
    Which they would hate.

So fear and habit checked their thoughts;
We must decode their secret jots
    For telltale signs.
From years and years with no redress
They only knew how to express
    The well-learned lines.

The patriarchal rule of thumb
Was all most knew and only some
    Failed to concede.
Not easy when so carefully taught
To come up with original thought
    And form a creed.

NEW RULES

Thou shalt not always be a lady
When men's dealings have been shady
    And you've been cheated.
You don't care who holds the door
And who minds anymore
    If men stay seated?

Thou shalt not always be polite
When it's a case of human right
    And self-respect.
Thou shalt not bow before a man
Who makes you less than what you can
    Be: proud, erect.

Thou shalt not meekly acquiesce
And answer with a simple yes
    To any census
Assuming women's unpaid work
Is valueless. That's knee-jerk
    In our consensus.

And so it goes, a bill of rights
Evolved o'er many sleepless nights
    But still obscured.
It isn't safe to be overt;
Better to mumble than to blurt,
    If uninsured.

In women's case the medium—
Her diary—seems like tedium;
    In the confines
Of old familiar adages
For safety's sake the message is
    Between the lines.

WHERE DO I FIT IN?

I read a definition once
About the basic difference
    Between a poet
And a playwright: the one forgets
All others for herself and lets
    The others know it

That she has special dispensation,
Free for fullest affirmation
    Of her true self.
A playwright, on the other hand,
Writing as others, taking the stand,
    Forgets her self.

So what has that to do with me?
Who am I supposed to be?
    (This causes stress.)
A person seeking self in others?
A person who is used by others?
    Yes, both, I guess.

I am both singer and the song.
Before you say that I am wrong
    And have no right,
Let me just call upon my muse
(If he agrees you can't refuse).
    He'll vouch despite

Your doubts re my ability
That I have real agility
    On paths untrodden.
I never stray far from the centre
When I have always had as mentor
    W.H. Auden.

A poet, but in early days
He tried his hand at writing plays.
    He does not faze me.
On him I wrote my Master's thesis;
His metric talent never ceases
    To amaze me.

This very poem that I write
Owes its metre and a quite
    Tricky rhyme scheme
To my mentor's influence.
What better for the pursuance
    Of my fond dream?

Thus I, as poet-playwright mixed,
Now find my writing muse betwixt
    A split domain:
The inner and the outer self.
Lest I end up upon the shelf
    There to remain,

I must be careful to be true
To mine own self as well as you,
    Dear diarists.
To you, my friends, I dedicate
And hope I can communicate
    Your interests.

To tell the truth, there's more at stake:
I hope with words to reawake
    Each woman's soul,
Distil the essence of her days,
Keep her inner flame ablaze,
    And play her role.

It's called dramatic monologue;
I'm writing it as epilogue—
    Hold back the night!
Left long unsung, then no one knows
A tune. By any name a rose
    Fades without light.

THE SELF

Whether or not she is detached,
And with a surface barely scratched,
    A woman tells of self.
No chorus, but a single voice,
She tells us of her daily choice:
    To thine own self

Be true. It starts out as a murmur
But gradually gets firmer,
    Growing bigger.
Awed by these women, loving too,
I see my role as trying to
    Match their vigour.

Consider me a secretary:
These voices speak aloud through me,
    But I'm no parrot.
I seek the essence of each life,
Of child or woman, maid or wife.
    Though quite disparate.

And when I get inside the mind
Of one such woman, then I find
    I learn much more
Than even she knew, or perhaps
It's in my mind that something snaps
    As I explore.

Let me just say that when I stumble
On a truth, foundations crumble.
    No one's to blame.
When honest woman sits to write
She's bound to set the world alight;
    Nothing's the same.

Bear with me then, and read between
These lines as if you've never seen
    The true distaff.
These diaries offer new sensations
And give us startling revelations—
    The better half.

Young Women

KATHIE GRAY (1864-?)

(a pseudonym for a woman who published a piece of her diary when she was old) In her old age "Kathie Gray" who had kept a diary all her life, revealed one year from her past.

I am neither Kathie nor Gray,
and yet I was colourful once,
young, unable to spell.
Now I cast a spell,
eyes in the back of my head,
rolling back time
rereading my past
back there in the light,
telling years like beads
on a string of time.

Editing sunshine I see at last:
I see through rheumy eyes
bright days forever summer:
Jessie my friend,
Mama my mentor
Harry my hero.

Jessie leaves,
I am lonely.
Mama is loving, reproving, ill,
I remorseful, repentant, rebellious.
Harry saves Sue in a daring dive
when she fell into water from a branch.
(Springing back, it lashed my eye.)
I am hurt.

I sit in darkness saving my eyes
safeguarding sight
smelling daylight savouring light
saving insight for my future,
which is dim.

Now the past is dim.
I pick it over pondering,
gray.

AGNES HELEN McGOWAN (1876-1919)

Daughter of the steward of the quarantine station on Partridge Island, St.John, New Brunswick, Nellie kept a diary for one year of her life, 1902, a significant one for her, as it turned out.

I only kept a diary but one year,
and that this one,
because I had paper and time
and it was meant to be.
Measles and smallpox stopped at our station
and we had deaths.

My sister Bessie nurses, older than me,
but I help, cooking cleaning disinfecting clothes
busy all the time when a ship is in
watching people.
Sick people need a lot of watching.

I tease her some, Bessie,
about Fred the station engineer who's sweet
on her, and they will marry—
not this year.
No time to court,
Sunday's like any other day.
Quarantine work kills plans and people.

Quarantine means you, too,
can't leave
can't go anywhere off the island,
stay where you are.
We sing play games.
Fred beats Bessie at Checkers
I beat Fred at Dominoes
Triangles is a standby Father likes.
Stormy winter evenings pass.
The station is safe.

On March 26 smallpox takes a Scotchman—
MacRae—his friends will never know.
Down on the east side by the sea the grave is,

and far away his mother, perhaps a wife
for all we know will wonder why he
no returns.

A Swedish girl with scarlet fever
and no English makes do, recovers.
A second lot: five measles, one spinal meningitis,
a little boy so sick, just two,
the fourth his parents lost, poor folk,
going miles away tomorrow
leaving their only son in a cold wet hole.
The thud of earth on a coffin lid
is a gruesome sound.
They left us a primrose
but it won't live.

Father is failing.

Summer is flowers and a rare visit
to town and Fred's young brother Jim,
a kid 18 with curly hair who gathers
lilacs that I lose.

In July I bake my birthday cake
but dare not mention age.
Pa is poorly, the weather so warm I swim—
first time since I was little.
More firsts follow:
jaunt in a hay-rack,
fortune in a tea-cup,
ride in a coach,
yellow fever on board,
first in St. John,
scarey.

I miss the boat and stay a week
missing the island.
Another quarantine lifted, safe
to return, but Father in pain.

Strange now to think he makes his last trip
off the Island, never to return.
One way. We too,
we cannot stay on the Island now.
Going by month-end, kill off the hens get ready
for Sunday in town.

Jim rows me down to look
so homesick for home
and Bessie is lonely on the Island
without us.

Have just come from watch night service
end of year solemn and sad. I wonder
how Bessie is on the Island tonight,
what a difference since last year.

p.s. She married the boy with the curly hair.

MARITAL RELATIONSHIPS

ANNE CLIFFORD (1590-1676)

Countess of Dorset, Pembroke and Montgomery, daughter and heiress of George Clifford, Earl of Cumberland. Married again after her first husband died, she left her second when she finally inherited her lands.

My "Day-by-Day book"

Two lords, no master.

They want my land
left me—rightful heir—by my father,
lacking sons, who died.

First spendthrift Dorset wants cash for land,
my land, appealing to the King (and I
to the Queen) to force me to let go.
I hold on.

The business lies ever between us
lying in and falling out—
grievously. He takes my child.
I weep.

I am like an owl in the desert

When he comes to visit we fall out
part for the night
over the business
my land.

Upon the 24th, being a Friday,
between the hours of six and nine
at night died my dear mother, at Brougham,
in the chamber where my father was born,
I being 26 and the child a month short of 2,
and she is to be buried in Westmoreland—
some contentment to my aggrieved soul.

Westmoreland is mine.
I will not part with it.
I will not part me from it.

Nothing will separate
it from me, it's mine
no matter how my lord's offended,
my land.

Ah well, he died.

Pembroke's my second
and still I will not
renounce my claim.

Not meek,
I inherit the earth my earth,
my land, and leave to live on
my land.

Passing time my intent
with faithful report
names people events:
who dined who played
who lost who won
who danced who prayed
when where.

Don't ask the why of it
or how. Don't ask me.

In time present time and past
all layer over
blur blend dim memory.
Without paper none
nothing exists nor me.

This day I dine.
I remember how this day was 60 years
I also dine. Yes.

Without my folk
within my fold.
Later nothing again.

Nobody dines
within or without
just me.

Nails—fingers & toes—hair too burnt
must be burnt in chimney in fire.
Nothing remains nothing of me.

Oh—memories—land
people prayers gifts land.

Falling out lying in
no one no lord no king
no one can will did ever take
my land from me
my land.

HANNAH CULLWICK (1833-1909)

Victorian scullery maid secretly married for 20 years to an upper-class English gentleman who loved her dirty and required her to keep a diary.

I'm Hannah Cullwick no man's bauble
though I am my Massa's slave (and he not mine?)

wear his padlocked chain around my neck
he holds the key—

cleaning takes time is all doing all in time
and paid for it kneeling on steps to scrub

kneeling to scrub my Massa's boots
playing games to show my love

he loves me in my dirt
I love to work not write he makes me write
    (hardest work I do)

I go to him in my dirt he likes that
hard work to get the black off

unseen in servant's dress no street stares
strong drudge invisible invulnerable

to dress a lady real risk no remedy
walking he takes my arm far from folks' eyes

we marry I lose the chain and lock
but who is free?

I hope he is not sorry nor I

PAULA MODERSOHN-BECKER (1876-1907)

German artist, torn between two loves and two lives: her husband and her art. Conventional behavior won; she died at the age of 33, of an embolism 18 days after giving birth to a daughter.

I have two loves so demanding
I'll die of wanting.

All my life I wait for life,
can hardly wait.
I serve two masters, served by neither:
art and love, oil and water mix not—
not in my day, unspent day.

Blank canvas, sketchy efforts, hard lines,
empty life, full arms embrace it all,
both, neither. My mouth and eyes agape
want it all. Patience!

I work on myself, gently weaving
threading love in and out of art and life,
thick with desire, snapped, unspent.

I think if I marry loneliness
will pass with someone there to feed
my soul. Mistake!

I'm lonely as a child,
illusion lost—worse—no hope left,
I need more.

I escape to art leaving love
leaving one love for my other love
passion obsession creation.
Easels are flimsy, husbands are frail,
no props at all.

Leave twice return twice creating
instead a child. Too soon forever
I am gone.

Pity!

EVELYN SCOTT (aka Elsie Dunn) 1893-1963

American novelist, more revered in her time than William Faulkner, Scott fled to Mexico with a married man and kept a diary of her experiences there, which she turned into the novel Escapade.

"He makes my eyes cool
with his smile "

I warm my hands
at his smoky heart

but I grow cold I grow cold
though I shall soon unfold
the rosebud within

I harden with despair
but he's no longer
hard up is all

How hard to feel the child
quicken, pushed
into life
while I am pushed
out of mine

As long as he sees me
I continue to be

He sees therefore I am

Will I always be?

SOPHIA TOLSTOY (1844-1919)
Everyone knows who the Russian novelist was but imagine being married to him!

If you expect a proper diary, a record:
"My Life with Leo Tolstoy,"
you will be disappointed.

I always write my diary when we quarrel,
that's why it's so big—
a tapestry of tantrums and toil,
melancholy and maladies,
dreariness and humdrum death.

How I wish I had something to say!

Lyovochka writes and writes, tears in his eyes
for his paper persons,
but none for us.
I copy his diaries and stories,
run his estates and servants and children.
I am a good nursemaid, nothing more,
while he plays man of the people.

How hard I work!

I am sick all the time, his fault,
working all the time, for him, bearing him
thirteen children thrust upon me (five died).
Eighteen—that's how old I was when Lev Tolstoy saw fit
to marry me, his doll,
and he thirty-four, debauched and worldly.
I dreamt of a pure person.

How I loved him!

I have nothing in the world but him,
no talent, no inner strength nor outer—nothing,
while he had all those women, loved them,
used them as he uses me. It is his past,
not his present, I cannot bear.

How jealous I am!

Why do people always think I am so happy?
People envy my happiness, what happiness?
What is happiness, what does happiness mean?
Don't let on. Men are bored by melancholy.

How I fear him!

When I am well and not pregnant—
how often I have been pregnant—
as if it were my fault I get pregnant—
stuck forever without love—when I'm pregnant.
When I'm well I enjoy physical pleasures,
disgusting as they are.

How I hate him!

He leaves me alone, a piece of household
furniture. I do not make him very happy.
It gets worse and worse.

How hard I try!

Try to recall good things:
music, the children playing piano,
walking in woods for violets,
flying kites, playing croquet,
lesson-time, sweet-time, coffee-time, snow-time—
death-time, too.

He doesn't suffer, he goes on writing,
I go on copying.
He is a genius.
I am not.
He is immortal.
I am not.

How I resent him!

The world sees a marvel
but I have to live with a man.

How I wish I were normal!

MA SEMBLABLE, MA SOEUR

HENRIETTE DESSAULLES (1860-1946)

A young French-Canadian who fell in love with the boy next door when she was a child. Forbidden contact with him, she kept a diary for comfort and companionship.

Toi, mon cher ami, mon journal,
you, my confidante, safekeeper,
discret, silent, sans jugement
or rebuke, you hold my present in your pages.
At fourteen, I perceive the present as forever,
the future flimsy fantasy, far off, forbidden.

Et toi, mon cher ami, my neighbour,
you, my confidant and listener,
aussi discret et silent, secretly sharing
What I fear to speak, and sometimes speaking
what I fear to share, you hold my present
in your fingers, my future in your heart.
At eighteen, you have too many years for me.
How can you see so clearly what I have fear
to know?

Et vous, Mama, not ma vraie mère,
you are no friend nor confidante
but keeper confining me,
keeping me from Maurice
who might as well be worlds away
instead of just next door,
All contact is forbidden, all smiles outlawed.
My dear Papa's wife, a step- away from love,
too busy with her babies to bother with me.
I am alone, and it feels like forver,
toujours seule.

Dis-donc, my paper partner, you must absorb
pain, blot tears, comfort & assuage,
assuring love and loyalty.
I dare not turn elsewhere:
not to my house and not next door
neither, no where. I wish...oui, and

dream aussi, sigh and shiver.
Forever is a long time coming.

Now, finalement, the future is forever
and here at last. How strange, quel merveil!
Maurice and I will marry and live
happily ever after.

Fear no more—time maybe, and,
some time,
in the future,
death.

I do not need you any more,
and so adieu

HESTER THRALE (PIOZZI) (1741-1821)

Contemporary and friend of Dr. Samuel Johnson, Hester Thrale, after a first marriage arranged by her mother, married for the second time for love—her daughters' dancing master.

My mother's child, my husband's wife—and she
chose him for me, I met him only once
before we wed—and then my daughters' care,
at least, I cared for them, gave them my life,
up to a point. But when they turned on me,
refused me love, denied my second spouse—
my first, my only choice—I flouted them
at last and wed to suit my heart's desire.

And then my friend, the learned doctor Sam,
whom Boswell followed like a puppy dog,
and whom I trusted, fed, and entertained
for years (I also writing down his words),
he, too, turned on me and gave me words
I didn't want to hear, expecting me
to be a nun when Mr. Thrale had died.
I can't. I can't be celibate, not now.
It's just too much to ask, and quite as hard
for me as for a man. I need to love.

And also, to be loved, a natural state
for most but not, alas, it seems, for me.
It comes as no surprise to me that I
am never thanked nor prized nor loved the way
I should be, never quite enough. I see
that in my lifetime I have ever been
a model of devotion, always more
tender of others' needs than they of mine,
and still they do not love me as I wish.

I work so hard. I try so hard to earn
my due of love, yet no one serves me as
I did Mother, but I must admit
she was perfection and I fall far short
of all her virtues. Nothing I can do
will ever equal her.

Why bother now?
The loss of Piozzi, my dearest love,
is all that hurts me now, and you, my book,
my only joy, my solitary friend,
my Confident, my comfort and my cheer,
and keeper of my every thought, now you
are all I have or ever will—or had,
if truth be told. Was it all a hoax?

SELF-ABSORPTION

MARY MACLANE (1881-1929)

Among the first of the personal diarists, Mary MacLane published her first wildly successful diary when she was 20 years old. A second popular diary followed failure as a novelist. This free spirit died at the age of 48, alone in a hotel room in Chicago.

After I stopped numbering days
I wrote to-morrow in my diary,
always to-morrow with a hyphen
as if it were a direction not a time.

Today it is today,
no to-morrows left
and nothing more to say.

I was my own creation a figment
of my imagination, an artist
on paper—you challenge that?
Ask me then what I created.

Me.

I used to be
interesting &
the most demanding
human being I knew.
My thoughts were all of me.

Today I don't think
I know anyone
including me.

External details, prosaic,
myriad, mystic, melted under
pen's steel nib, molten.
I was on fire, alight with words.
The world put out my fire.

Sensate sensible sensitive I
saw touched tasted

the tactile world hungering
all the way
wanting it all
until today.

Four radishes two crackers
a thin glass of water,
then my anchorite lunch.
Today I am less lavish
and do without the radish.

Once I found bliss
in a boiled potato, cold.
Today my shelf is cold.

I've used up everything:
food words shock revelations
no surprises left
nothing. I am bereft.

Once I prayed for death
haply to overtake me
before menopause.
Today I'm forty-eight,
considered odd.

What did I mean?
What did God?

SEI SHONAGON (963-?)

Sei Shonagon was a court lady in tenth-century Japan. In her Pillow Book she recorded a few of her favourite and unfavourite things.

My Pillow Book's not
 for looking

Like embroidery
 the other side's
 squalid

See through me
 colours memories

Sense through me
          delicious aroma
         lute sound
          purple flowers
 paper thread
         splendid

Lovers depart
 more eager than I
 to leave
 this ragged world
 pulling on cloaks
 azalea-yellow or
 vermilion over white

I must be first
   or not

DOROTHY WORDSWORTH (1771-1855)

Sister of the poet, William Wordsworth, Dorothy served as cook and amanuensis and opened her heart and diary to her brother until she went dotty.

His sister,
I keep my journal
to give him pleasure
not to quarrel with myself
nor with him
my heart his home

We walk
I note weather people views
We talk
sometimes Coleridge comes with news

If sometimes I weep for him
so many reasons
William says
"nervous blubbering"

I bake
both pies and bread
cook wash iron
take tea
feed beggars
copy poems
read write letters
this journal
I listen watch

Our favourite birch tree:

"...yielding to the gusty wind
with all its tender twigs,
the sun shone upon it
and it glanced in the wind
like a flying sunshiny shower.
It was a tree in shape
with stem and branches

but it was like a spirit of water.

The other birch trees that were near it
looked bright and cheerful,
but it was a creature
by its own self among them."

Fire flutters
watch ticks
I hear nothing save
William's breathing
now and then he turns
a new leaf

We feast with silence
the least sound
our sustenance
voice of the air
feeding creation:
frost flowers fog
stones stars sky
birds beggars boats—
    "the moon a perfect boat a silver boat"
We sleep

I drop thoughts like purls
in my knitting he picks up
for his poems

"What a beautiful thing God has made winter to be
by stripping the trees and letting us see
their shapes and forms.
What a freedom it seems to give
to the storms."

William composes
no poet I
privileged to be amanuensis
I copy keep watch
not a poet

no matter what you think
William
William's the one to live
to live for

"Monday was a frosty day,
and it has been frost ever since.
It is today Christmas Day Saturday 25th December 1802.
I am 31 years of age.
—It is a dull frosty day."

RITUAL CODES

EMILY HAWLEY GILLESPIE (1838-1888)

This Iowa farm wife kept a detailed diary all her life but never revealed her "secret to be burried" [sic].

Pondering on the past, wondering what may be
my future lot,
writing in the present. I,
Emmie E. Hawley, noting tasks and weather,
do not tell all. I will remember.
Clowdy. [sic]

Work for hire, sew for hire,
teach some too, then hire out as niece.
Moving from Michigan to Iowa to old Uncle Henry's inn.
Cold as fury.

Can it be that next week
Emmie is to be a bride?
Emily Hawley Gillespie, wife of James.
Working for love now, not free,
I have become we.
James is my best friend.
Fair.

Two children, Sarah and Henry
(Sarah's twin died) and that's plenty.
I pity women who have too many,
and so I count: !!!
(Oh! Oh! Oh! means no child this month).
Rainy.

Pleasure past, I count blessings,
do what I can, do what I must,
if things would only stay clean.
All is well.
Warm.

And thou, dear journal,
my only confidante,
thou dost not know every secret.

James says I may write in my diary but
to have warmer feet when I come to bed.
Coldest day this winter.

Such good children, a very kind husband,
this world's not a dream but calm reality.
Warm.

I only wonder that more women must not be taken
to the asylum, farmers' wives.
No company, hard work, their children
their only joy.

15th Anniversary.
Pleasant.

James is cross, one of his moods.
I like to make home pleasant.
Shower.

Almost a hermit, always at home,
I must not give up.
The children are here.
Foggy.

I sometimes think woman
is but a mere tool.
Warm like spring.

Twenty in my mind though forty today
and my hair is near half grey.
May I never lose my wits
as some my age have done.
Cold.

Ever at home, never give up.
Anniversary today—how changed since then.
Children spared to us.
Pretty cold.

Well I remember castles in the air,
perhaps well as it is.
I often wish I might never be sad.
And then I get mad, yes mad.
Forgive and forget.
Awful warm.

Work has no end, I can't give up.
Now Sarah helps, together we work.
The worse we feel, the harder we work.
Snow.

Woman is lovely until she fails
and then she's in the way.
All men find fault with what is done
and angry if it's not.
Warm.

Out in the barn with a rope,
James in one of his fits—
such a trial. Trust God.
We're spared another day.
Warm.

Christmas, no presents, lonely indeed,
going nowhere, no one coming.
Beautiful day.

Birth day. 44.
No one remembers.
Keep up good courage Emmie!
Sprinkle.

James is being ugly to his horses.
Too mean to tell.
I sit on the floor by Sarah's bed,
writing. Fear not
but trust in Providence.
Mud.

Twentieth anniversary.
I burned up my life on the hot stove.
Then my hands were like a lily
now a faded rose, 'tis all right,
I have a daughter and a son.
Thy will be done.
Fair.

When a man lays his hands hold
of his wife & children
I think 'tis time
something was done.

It must be a real disease people get,
so full of some undefinable thing
they must explode.
Try to believe 'tis natural.
All is not bitter.

Try not to be nervous,
it makes everything bad.
Bad spells for James
make bad head for me.
My health seems good only dizzy
in my head. Tired. Not pleasant
to keep still and only listen.
Dear Old Journal, none but you.
Pleasant.

Valentines Day, James said
a kiss is good as anything
and gave it me.
We are growing old,
nearer so much nearer
to our time to leave this world.
Snow & Cold.

He said, "Emily, I believe you mean
to kill me some time let me know when
so I can meet my God prepared."

I said, “You have no reason.”
Riding alone with him in the dark.

Sarah and I write in our journals,
Father in bed. I am so tired,
hands almost useless as to feeling.
Relief in tears, Thy will be done.
Rain all day.

Henry and Sarah dare not leave me
alone with him.
There is no reason in him.
I have been obliged to deed away my home,
not sad to leave, long his wish.
I am sorry my love
or friendship
is broken. He killed my turkeys.
Third time, no accident.
Dizzy.

With a chair at the head of the stairs
the noise will wake me
if he comes up. Keep safe.
I wish we might have lived
happily ever and we have
compared with many.
A long winter is before us.

How grand it would be to live
not for mere life. All alone.
60° right here not six feet from the stove.
Snow.

Work is the same
whether sick or well.
So tired, such is life.
Snowing.

It is nice to be a man if one is a man.

He wants me to sleep with him.
I do not feel as I did for such talk.
Again this morning: "Are you awake?"
He said he was going to get into bed with me.
No!
Not to lie back in the cold.
He would not speak all morning.
We part.
Left ear ringing.

Raving maniac,
he chases Henry with the pitchfork.
I have written many things but the worst
is a secret to be burried
when I shall cease to be.
Can't walk.

Ah, marriage is a lottery.
False tongues until after one is married.
O for equal rights and man and woman
get out of the old ruts.
Warm.

[NEW VOICE: JOURNAL IN SARAH'S HAND]

I write in Ma's journal what she says:
Sarah is here and cares for me
the best she can.
Henry is gone. James comes often,
hard for him alone up there.
Blizzard of drifting snow.

Ma's work is nearly done.
And all is well.
Snow.

MARGARET GRAY (MRS. ARTEMAS LORD) 1845-1941

Margaret Gray began her first diary when she was 18 and kept one for 30 years, missing four days due to sea-sickness on board a ship bound for England, and a week or two after the birth of each of her seven children; the first two died young.

I live by routine and duty
give pleasure to others (and me?)
Small disappointments teach one
patience for big ones.
I will not
fail.
God willing—Deo Volente.

A busy life of work I do not shirk
at home and kirk
enjoying sermons visits talks
and walks with Artie
and gardening sewing helping
servants cook—but not the cleaning
except in spring.
I will
keep on,
God willing—D.V.

I visit my babies' tombstones
ever marking milestones
of the lives that might have been.
To others they're unseen,
but they keep on growing older in my mind.
They don't grow old in Heaven.
I will not
dwell in sadness, D.V.

I do get tired, headaches rage
when others' babies die. I age,
eyes ache with sewing
and my dear sister-friend marries off the Island.
I will
see her again, D.V.

Then rheumatism palpitations
colds and flu storms and cold.
The seasons pass and I grow old.
I will not
be afraid, D.V.

WORK

LOUISA MAY ALCOTT (1832-1888)

Nineteenth-century American writer, who took care of her family with her pen. Her mother used to read her diary and comment.

Like a spider, feel like a spider,
busy spinster, spinning yarns like a spider,
spinning my brains out for money
dreading debt more than the devil.

    Remember, dear girl, that a diary
    should be an epitome of your life.

Mother, I never forget.
You work Father talks,
I catch money in my web
head-money blood money.
I am my parents' only son.

    Remember, dear girl

I know what they'll say:
Mother is Marmee I am Jo
all my little women mere copies from life.
Never liked girls much or knew many
except my sisters.
Boy's spirit under my bib and tucker
mind too rampant for my body
writing machine.

    an epitome of

If I weren't so busy spinning I could write
something good
something real
something lasting.
I must be useful make money be famous.
Fame is expensive, cobwebs get in.
I ask for bread and get a stone—
a pedestal for sightseers.
Need to be alone

to spin like a spider.

your life

Life is words
life is hard work.
So tired tethered to my web
I want not to ache
to be peaceful quiet free.
Life is rather a burden.

MARY BOYKIN CHESNUT (1823-1886)

A Southern flower with a whim of iron, Mrs. John Chesnut kept a diary recording the news and her feelings about the Civil War.

Like a spider, that's what I am
jest a-spinnin and a-spinnin
usin up my own entrails
unable to do a thing!

Powerful talk—we all do that.

This war, I declare—
those Yankees are damn liars—
be the death of us my husband too
JC's goin to war makes me
miserable—not one word!
I know he ought.

War is so stupid so are men.

We all led quiet lives too ready for excitement
but this! All confusion
livin in rooms from place to place
always waitin for some new face
for news for somethin—for anythin!—
to happen.

Some old man said it'd take 40 years
to get rid of the he-roes.
JC's goin in the Senate how can I say
go in the Army? Wish it was in my power.
Everybody's electioneerin and dare not
speak truth.
I wonder if
in the 1000s of compliments I garner
there is a grain of truth.

Why was I born so frightfully ambitious?

Clever too, much good it does,

stupid & feverish & sleepy & head-achey
and Mistah Chesnut in a bad humour,
wantin to be a congressman.
The papers, licensed liars, don't care what's true
spreadin hateful and hideous falsehoods
'bout the battles and us retreatin
and them fleein and us too frightened to pursue
and then our handlin of wounded & prisoners—
all lies! And every paper reminds us
women are to be violated, ravished and humiliated—
all sighs.

These times make all women feel humiliation.

I sit and knit, all us knitters
contemplatin the world at large
while none but noodles seem to be in charge.

I was glad seein JC's name
in print once more
the world seems forgettin him
but oh the dyin death and dyin on every side
the ground struck from under our feet
enough to shake one's nerves—
cruel fate!
How eagerly we cling to hope and good news—
too late.

I have done with schemin
all my darlin plans upset.
I knit & gossip and thank God—
in public—
for all his mercies and yet and yet and yet

If I had been a man
in this great revolution
I had either
been killed at once
or made a name
& done some good

for my country—
O my country.

My meddlin & advisin days are over.

My negroes now
free citizens
humble & lovin & fearful
ask to remain not pleased
at sudden freedom
but they will go—after a while.
JC hires them for wages
while he waits to be arrested.
He will neither hide nor fly
and I
of ladies most deject & wretched
that suck'd the honey of his music vows
wait with him
for the sword to fall.

It has already fallen.

TRAVEL

ISABELLA BIRD (1831-1873)

One of the British intrepid travellers, this migratory Bird explored the Colorado Rockies alone on a horse.

They admire pluck in a woman
ride your own fashion,
do as you like—
cavalier? Why not?

Blissful alone astride
in scenery made for superlatives
wearing my Hawaiian riding dress
    with semi-fitted jacket
    skirt to the ankles
    full Turkish trousers
    gathered into frills over the boots
serviceable feminine
dust cloak over all
well-worn white umbrella for the sun
polished inside of watch case my mirror
constantly assaulted
by beauty:

elastic air
dense pine below blue sky above
heaven-piercing peaks
slake my soul exceed my dreams.

My goal was Estes Park
tumbling on a trail
struggling up a gulch
poised on a precipice
lost, I guided my guide back down
better off alone
having fun

It's a dry cold they say you don't feel
but in a blizzard hard
to remember or see
eyelashes stuck with snow

picking one eyelid open
with one ungloved finger
lost but for my horse
who had enough sense to come in
out of the storm

Sheltered blanketed
with snow
making myself agreable
to hosts too poor to leave
I left, moved on

Estes park at last
huddling for the winter
with a few pounds of flour and two youths
who burrowed for wood while I tended
the fire and mended
my threadbare Hawaiian riding dress
tried to keep memory warm
ink and fingers frozen
fun and life elusive
like Mountain Jim—

Feared, hiding from the law
for some unspeakable crime—
my friend talked more
shared less
than either of us wanted

When I left I left
a part of me
taking nothing

I'm a tourist at heart.

LADY LOUISA LAMBTON, LADY DURHAM (1797-1841)

Wife of the first governor general of Canada, Lady Durham accompanied her husband, albeit reluctantly, when Lord Durham was sent out to solve the problems after the 1837 Rebellion. She kept a diary of her brief sojourn in Canada.

I suspected the weather all along
not often very pleasant, the changes
too sudden. I imagined it
a disagreeable place to live in, great plagues—
the servants, so hard to please.
And then the want of furniture
and conversation, trying to offend no one.
Without music I can't think what we might have done.
No one listens.

Who in her right mind
would want to go to Canada? My dear—
the women! Dreadful,
more smartly dressed than I expected but the fear!
Picking up the wrong forks—
one ate jelly with her knife—
they drank 36 dozen of champagne, silent.
So toilsome to be charming all the time.
When I think of my Mary here, it's a crime.
We're never alone.

And He is never out of uniform, official,
receiving salutes, giving dreadful dinners,
pacifying all the time, a formidable business.
Receptions, levées, and balls,
pageants, programs and ceremonies—so difficult
to keep from laughing, such people!
I assure you the ladies are no sinecure.
The effort to be cordial palls.
No wonder He gets headaches and stumbles and falls.
The heat is oppressive.

Ah, but Niagara Falls!
Never, never, never, never
have I seen anything so—they said
you'll either love them or hate them I love them—
the most stupendous, sublime & beautiful spectacle
in Creation, the face
of everything changed: hope soared
doubts flown gloom gone difficulties vanished
No longer did I feel banished.
I hated to leave.

We left (not there for pleasure)
Toronto lay in wait—
and another headache for Him
and people inspections addresses
a dinner a levée and tour—so ended 2 days
of duties to strangers and frightful fatigue.
And all the while the dreadful intrigue,
malice in the House.

His enemies not here but at home
changing old orders:
mediate, He was told
pacify reconcile appease
close the breach heal the rupture
spread balm pour oil on the heads
of rebels French & English alike—never alike,
very distinct.
The problem:
how to deal with 500 political prisoners leftover
from the 1837 Rebellion, 2/3 already released
and how He wished the rest released.
He needed rest.

Come to trial in Lower Canada
the rebels would get off.
No sense in a hanging jury
no sense in smiling amnesty
no sense in dissension. He solved the problem
by banishing to Bermuda

8 ringleaders and pardoning the rest.
I think it was all for the best.
The Queen et al did not agree.

All comes to an end, good and bad.
They named a tea after my father Earl Grey
but He—Lambton—my lord and husband,
He was sent home in disgrace
and I with Him, who never wanted
to go in the first place.

The posting was the punishment.

JANE ELLICE (d. 1864)

Wife of Lord Durham's secretary, Edward Ellice, the lively young Scotswoman, Jane Ellice, and her husband accompanied the Durhams to Canada where the Ellice suffered a rebellion of their own on their estate at Beauharnois.

I promised my father-in-law a record of the trip:
beginning bonnie ending bleak.
I danced across the ocean with my sister
Edward danced attendance on the Durhams
as he must.

Lord D's not easy
(she calls him He)
barking orders and his shins
on duty not much fun
but he is just.

She, too, serious
finding people I find funny tedious
appalled at appetites
for food and life—
I'm not so august.

My greatest trial (until the end)
not by fire but by bugs
torment worse than heat or people
unseen foe raising irritation
swelled and fussed.

At Beauharnois just days before departure
rebellion split our air and lives
Tina with me Edward elsewhere
imprisoned and hungry—
scarcely a crust.

Survival poses questions we can't
answer for ourselves or others
Fate hangs us in the balance
and when it's over
I have lost trust.

ANNE LANGTON (1804-1893)

An Englishwoman who settled in the Bobcaygeon area, Ontario, Canada, with her brother and family, and kept a diary-cum-letters back home about her experiences in the colonies.

Get a notion
to cross an ocean
begin again, gain a
new perspective,
hither to the hinterland
by sea by land by—
how to begin to convey?

The Falls are not disappointing,
I am: to come so far
and bring me with me.

Mother, Father, Aunt and I
help my brother John
near Sturgeon Falls, Ontario—
make a home and carry on,
so much to be done.
So much has been done.

Reality matches mind's eye—
almost—matches mind's hope
of what I had expected,
but for the wood,
the woods—to walk in and to clear.

I will sketch when I find a good scene.

A winter's chopping will improve the view,
and a good burning.
(Then stumps stain ground water,
decaying roots spread rot.)
Back logs best for the fire—
no wonder they call these backwoods.

No seasoned wood for building

but season's worth for burning.
A washhouse, boiler, and an oven—
great comforts all—consume
a multitude of wood.

We gobble wood, a glowing pyre,
Canadian maple, two trees a day,
and let the chips fall where they may,
to heat, to cook, to eat, to sleep—
perchance to dream, ay, there's the rub—
for in the night the warmth subsides.
The water seldom freezes overnight
in the recess by the fire, otherwise—
my blood circulates, if nothing else.

When once no chance
of being too warm
perhaps a chance
of being warm enough.

I have been as cold in England
but for my aching finger tips,
cracking thumb and index deeper...
more dreadful than cold is winter's length....
So be it. My thoughts run hot and cold.

Washing baking candle-making
prized far above
sewing sketching reading.
I have learned many skills perforce.
Used to be a lady, gentlewoman,
merely woman now not gentle—
old maid—
never (thanks be) old bachelor.
Scrubbing is a skill men lack.

No good help:
too young when they come,
they leave too soon
to marry and burn

more wood, bear babies, labour and toil.
I say it, may as well (who will mind?),
woman is a slave in this country.
In the absence of all domestics
ladies luxuriate, easier without,
paying the price of refinement.

It's not the work
it's the silence.
Solitude not servitude
does in a woman. Forest seclusion
sounds more poetic than it is.
We must have company sometimes.

Then from rotting decaying fetid stumps roots sloughs
the ague begins, with its death grippe—
whole families down—
fever, nothing to be done.
Men's work suspended but how to live
without women's work?
No bread, no butter, no clean clothes,
true hardship.

Father gone before, then Mother died
and Aunt six weeks apart. I too,
too ill to stay, departed.
John wed and I, devoted,
returned to help.

Now I am Aunt, deaf, old,
keeping warm in Canada.

ORDEALS

JANINA BAUMAN (b. 1927)
Polish Jewish teenager, keeping alive in the Warsaw ghetto, staying out of the death camps, hiding out in WWII

They stole my life
but I am survivor

12 years old in Konstancin, Poland, in 1939,
daughter of Jewish doctor, decided
to keep diary and got on with it
the first six days of war.

Father moved us to Warsaw to be safe,
evacuated his hospital
hours before siege—gone forever—
leaving Mother Sophie and me.

So mole's life began
breathless in basement
as bombs fell.

Ghetto like freedom
after cellar:
attending school of sorts,
giving my sandwich to beggars,
digging in cemetery—compost of corpses—
planting life, stench of death
from mass graves staining my brain
forever. Never
anywhere to go, never
alone but alive.

Time's up.
Now we play Cat & Mouse
crouched in cupboards
cloaked in closets
confined in cabinets
then running running running
marathon of fear
    and boredom:

missing train for Treblinka
evading papers for camp
hiding in somebody's kitchen
stealing clothes that are damp
scrounging food to survive on
poking in other folks' homes
living off dead peoples' relics
—like Christians in old catacombs?

Corruption in my soul,
I care not a damn.

Keeping diary again
writing reading searching for food
still running. Is there reason why
I keep running for my life?

Assuming it was worth it,
assuming identity...

I am Christian virgin
hidden in wall with fifteen people
four days and out—
all the way out.

Mother, Sophie and I left the Warsaw ghetto
on 25 January 1943

Still learning survival
watching people die
inside and out.

Out of money at last, dead
but for one diamond
—T.B. or not T.B.—
nothing wrong
good food clean air sweet freedom
won't cure.
Hiding in others' lives
I smoke and write on and on and on and on

till suddenly
Warsaw burns.

I hide diaries
in hole in floor in ruined house
and run. "Not Jewish," I say,
"Armenian."
For some reason Nazis tolerate Armenians,
we get away.

Now I am Christian in Zielonki
with peasant family called Pietrzyk
in love with Virgin Mary.
Have I been infected? No.

I belong to Jews because I have suffered
one of them.
Suffering has made me Jewish.

No more waiting, I want to live now.

FANNY BURNEY (1752-1840)

(Madame D'Arblay)

English novelist, maried an officer in Napoleon's army, experienced the first recorded mastectomy, in 1811, by an army surgeon, without anaesthetic.

A Mastectomy
at the hands of Baron Larrey (1766-1842),
Napoleon's famous army surgeon
[30 September 1811]

Not to trouble, as my spouse would say.
A living hand writes this, surviving.
Silent till now, I'm still among the living,
telling all. Only a year ago—
more torment spent in fear than physical
increase—a small pain niggling in my breast,
a large one keeping pace within my heart—
both grew alarmingly, alarming me.

D'Arblay watched and urged me to consult
Dr. Jouart, physician of a friend.
He failed outright to set me at my ease.
Acting on his orders I grew worse.
Monsieur d'A insisted that I see
another—M. Dubois, accoucheur to
the Queen. And finally it dawned on me—
a present danger, fear no less increased
when D'Arblay failed to come to me at once,
spending instead too many minutes with
the sage. And when he came, such shocking looks,
so haggard in appearance that I knew
the news was bad: A small operation
was all, but necessary to avoid
evil consequences! Oh, too dire,
but direr still the pains as they increased,
the hardness of the spot affected harder
yet, but tender—symptoms too overt
to be ignored.

My horror of the knife
was overwhelming, yet there seemed no choice.

M. Dubois referred me to Baron
Larrey, a genius in his field, who gave
me some relief. Although I suffered pain,
the fits were shorter and more rare and I
could go about my daily rounds with ease—
in short, was well, and my alarm abated.

Then sad events intruded on my life—
the illnesses and deaths of some dear friends—
and I, not stong enough for sorrow, changed
all for the worse. "Et qu'est il donc arrive?"
dismayed Larrey inquired when he came.
The hardness would not thaw nor yet resolve
into a dew. And so the knife must fall.

He promised me at least four hours warning
for the blow, and so I did prepare.
I made my Will, and tried—I swear I tried—
to set my mind at ease. (My soul was slow.)

But then it came, the fateful time with but
two hour's notice and the need
to hide from D'Arblay what I must endure.
He stood before me as I read the note
informing me of imminent release
(one way or another). I took my time
in reading while I caught my breath to plan.
My fear was greater that he learn the truth
than any terror of what fate befall.

I asked an ally to devise a task
for him to go off to perform (and he,
thus forced to leave me on my own,
sat down and sobbed, or so I later learned).

I ate a crust of bread, I know not how,
and sent word by a maid that I'd be set

at one o'clock, and sent my husband on
his way. He'd scarcely left when Dubois
and the rest all came but I renewed
my plea for one o'clock, and they agreed.
I had to make arrangements for my mate,
not knowing what would happen later on.

But then, when I was ready, he was not—
M. Dubois. 'Twas then my turn to wait
two hours of an endless time in fear.
(I could not write because my arm was weak.)
I strolled and saw the salon all prepared
for my ordeal and I recoiled but then
returned to look again, no turning back.

The sight of sponges, bandages, and lint
made me a little sick, but I kept pace
with fear by walking back and forth until
I was inert, insensate by the hour
of three. Before I faced it, I took pen,
defying my poor arm, and wrote a note
to him, my love, a few words, just in case.
The doctors came on then and greeted me.
I drank some wine and entered the salon.

Seven men in black surrounded me.
Why so many? and without leave?
I could not speak a word while Larrey sent,
to my dismay, for beds—two mattresses—
when he had promised just a chair
was all I'd need—and also an old sheet.
I then began to tremble violently
with horror at the preparations more
than from the fear of future pain. I stood
suspended while I looked around in vain
at door and windows for escape. I called
my maid who wept while two attendants hung
about the door, transfixed. "Let all those
women go!" Dubois gave order and
his voice recovered mine: "No!"I cried.

"Qu'elles restent! I want them all to stay with me."
The maid, however, and one nurse ran off.
I asked the other to approach and she
obeyed, and so did I, although I tried
resisting orders to remove my robe
which I had meant to keep.

"Can you," I cried,
"have any feeling for what seems to you
a trivial act, this simple operation?"

Dubois then stammered, "Trivial, madame?"
and stopped, unable to go on, disturbed.
He tore a bit of paper into shreds
while Dr.Larrey kept aloof, but pale.

I knew that danger hung above my bed
as I lay back and Dubois placed a cloth
upon my face, a cambric handkerchief.
But I could see right through it and I saw
the seven men, the nurse, and then bright steel.
I shut my eyes. Long pause and silence then
as they made signs, I guess, and planned their moves.

Then Larrey broke the pause and asked out loud—
did he expect response?—"Who will hold,"
he asked, "Qui me tiendra ce sein?"

No one replied but I was fired again
by fear and saw the hand of Dubois rise
describing with his finger a straight line
from top to bottom of my breast, and then
a cross, and thirdly in a circle—No!
I started up, threw off my veil and cried,
"Who will hold this breast for you, c'est moi!"
And I it was who held it up for him
to cut, explaining all the while my fear
that they would take it all. They heard me out,
then gently placed me as before and spread
the veil upon my face again. Alas,

how vain my plea. I saw once more the finger
describe the cross and circle in the air.
I shut my eyes once more and giving up
all hope, relinquishing all watching, I lay
resigned to fate, and waited for the knife,

What torturing pain that then ensued I can't
describe, when dreadful steel plunged deep into
my breast. It cut through veins and nerves and flesh.
No need to urge me not to hold back cries
for I began a scream that cut through hearts
and walls as long as that knife cut through me.
I almost marvel that it rings not yet.

Once the cut was made, the knife withdrawn,
the air rushed in like barbed and pointed darts
tearing the edges of the wound and then
I felt the knife again cutting against
the grain, across resisting flesh. I knew
it tired the man who held the knife because
he changed from hand to hand to give it rest.

I thought I must have died. I closed my eyes
so tight the eyelids seemed indented in
my cheeks. A second time the knife withdrew
and I concluded that the surgery
was done, but no—the cutting was renewed,
and worse, the aim now being to detach
the bottom of this dreadful gland from parts
to which it did adhere, and then, my God!
I felt the knife against the bone—the breast
bone—raking, rasping, scraping, scouring.

Though speechless in my torture yet I heard
Larrey inquire if more was yet to cut.
I felt Dubois's finger in the air.
Although he did not touch. I felt him point
another spot and then began the knife
again to scrape, demanding that my flesh
should yield the final atom of decay.

Even now—a full nine months have passed—
I'm sick at going on with this acccount.
It lasted twenty minutes, that ordeal,
including all the treatment and the shrouds.

I never moved nor stopped them from their work,
nor spoke, save once or twice to simply say
while they applied the dressings,

"Ah, Messieurs!
que je vous plains!" and it was true, I did
feel for them and their concern for me.

I fainted twice, at least I think I did,
because there are two spaces in my mind,
two chasms where I can't recall events,
a kind of gap in continuity.

They carried me to bed, too weak to walk,
my limbs were limp, my face devoid of hue.
The movement caused my eyes to open and
I saw Larrey with face as pale as mine,
all streaked with blood and looking down at me
with equal parts of horror, grief, and fear.

Once safe in bed, I saw my dear d'Arblay
and we thank God together for my health.

MEDICAL REPORT by Baron Larrey's "Chief Pupil"

Madame d'Arblay a subi hier à trois heures quarante-cinq L'extirpation d'une tumeur Cancéreuse du volume du poing et adhérente au muscle grand Pectorale et Dévelopée dans le sein droit. À dix heures la malade est étonnée du bien être qu'elle éprouve-M. Larrey la trouve sans fièvre....

THERESA GOWANLOCK (b. 1865?)

A Canadian bride from Ontario who moved west with her new husband and was a victim of the Duck Lake Rebellion. Taken prisoner, she lived for two months in the camp of Big Bear in the spring of 1885.

Newly wed, inept and full of hope,
I leave my father's house to pioneer,
departing from Ontario by rail,
by boat, by rail, by rail until we reached
Swift Current in Saskatchewan
and there it ended. No more steam.

Then on we go by buckboard living under
canvas, making tea and setting fire
to the prairie grass—an accident—
but we enjoyed it, such a stunning sight!

I stopped at Battleford six weeks while he,
my husband, went to build the mills and store
and—best of all—a home for both of us,
not a palace but a cabin made
of logs. It is enough. I don't want more.

We're off again—another camping trip.
I cope with candles in a tent and eat
nice fish, nice prairie hens, sleep well and hope
Frog Lake is getting close. I meet new friends,
the Delaneys, man and wife, just two
miles north of where we stop at last—Frog Creek,
my home. I settle home, not homesick now.

Our closest neighbours, Big Bear's band, speak Cree
and trade us whitefish twice a week for tea,
and sugar, prints and more, all from the store.
At New Year's they all want a kiss which I
would rather die than do, in fact, will not.
These people do not sit on chairs they squat
down on their feet, too tiring for me.
They're idle folk but don't deserve to starve.
Delaney and my husband feed them all.

Even when the governor says stop
They do not.

Weather crisp but dry;
you hardly feel the cold, and so the win-
ter passes by until the time of blood
and death—cruel death. My life too is gone
with my beloved, passing like a dream
before this horror that will never leave
my heart. Never.

I must relive it now.

The news from Duck Lake reached us at the end
of March: a rising and a fight. Big Bear
says he will not join them, claiming peace,
making April fools of all of us—
safe, we think. That night we sleep in peace,
staying at Delaneys' just in case.

The warning comes too late: our horses gone
and Big Bear's men besiege the house and take
our arms. But after breakfast we all go
to church, and they come too, inside and out.

My husband says "You'd better wear your shawl,
It's very cold. Perhaps it's not for long."

They go through all the stores and steal the lot,
and take us up the hill towards their camp.
Half-way there we hear the shots; they kill
three men. I cry, my husband takes my arm
and says, "Dear wife, be brave unto the end,"
and then they fire again and he falls down
beside me, reaching out, and I fall down
and bury my face on his as his life ebbs.
The next shot would be mine and I am braced,
thinking I will join him soon, but no-

my death is not to be. I have a while.

They pull me from my dying husband's side
but I refuse to leave. How can I leave
him there for those cruel men to dance around?
I beg to stay, but I am pulled away.
I see Delaney fall and she is pulled
as well. I still look back to where he lies-
beloved husband dying-and I think
my heart will break. I would have died with him
and been at rest, but that is not allowed.

Half conscious, I am led a captive, forced
through brush and bush in water to my waist
to Big Bear's camp, cold and in despair.
I see Mrs. Delaney and I ask
to speak to her but am denied and pushed
into a tepee where a friendly squaw
takes off my shoes and helps me to get dry.
I cannot eat but huddle in the smoke
and then the braves come in the tent and dance
and some are wearing my dear husband's clothes
and I consider that my end is near
and wait for the result while they all yell
and swing their clubs and knives, while I am calm.

I was unconscious for a long long time
but when I wake to feel a woman bathe
my face the water is so cold I know
I am alive. I learn a half-breed man
called Peter Blondin bought me and my friend
Mrs. Delaney for a horse and cash—
some thirty dollars—not as kind as you
might think. He wanted me to go with him
but I refused and he was mad and tried
to injure me and treated me with shame.
The husband of the one who bathed my face,
a man called Pritchard, who is kinder than
the rest, protected me, and I stay in

their tent and will not go with Blondin when
he asks again.

Then Big Bear too
comes in our tent and says "I'm sorry now."
He cries and says it's not his fault, at least
we will not starve or bear the injuries
that Indians do at white men's hands. He says
he will protect us but his braves come in
and dance and brandish knives and tomahawks
while looking at us wickedly. "Oh let
them live," says Pritchard begging for our lives.
"For God's sake let the women live!"

To tell the truth, to die is least of all my fears;
I know a fate far worse than death awaits
if ever we should leave the tent. I shake
each time they enter expecting death or worse.
A brave stands up and pointing to the sky,
"We swear," he says, "by God, that we'll not hurt
these two, that we will let these women live."
They do not keep their word, but come at night
to take us to their tents. The Pritchards wake
and trade their goods for us: dishes and blankets
and Mrs. Pritchard takes the best one off
her bed, and they go off and after that
the half-breeds keep us safe from night to night
for we have not a single minute's safety.

The Saturday of Easter we appeal,
requesting decent burial: to lay
to rest our husband's bodies at the church.
They place them with the priests' beneath the floor
and then set fire to the church and dance
around it, screaming as they watch it burn
clear to the ground.

I hear our husbands' bodies
are charred beyond belief or recognition.
I think my heart will break again and weep

and when they see my tears they say, “That’s right,
you cry plenty. We have killed
your husbands and we’ll soon have you.”

On the 6th of April they attack
and take Fort Pitt without a single loss.
They take white prisoners and bring them to
the camp. What a relief it is to see
white folk again! I give a woman tea.

Soon after they move camp about two miles
from Frog Lake. We walk through mud and water
while they in warm coats laugh and jeer astride
their horses so we laugh as well, Mrs.
Delaney and I, pretending to have fun.
I see Blondin in my husband’s coat
and shiver in my shawl. He laughs and asks
if I would like his coat and I say “No,
for I don’t mind the cold as much as you.”

My heart is full of grief and apt to break
and all I wish for is my death—just close
my eyes and go to God—and yet I live.
I only eat to keep myself alive
for if I flag they’ll make me leave the tent
and that will be a harrowing end of me.

The Pritchards make us work to earn our keep;
my friend and I cut wood, haul water, cook
and sew, using cloth and the lace I made
last year and folded carefully away.
It’s in my trunk they stole, with other things.
I watch their children play with treasures that
my mother gave to me, and when they break
them say no word. And pictures of my friends
are torn and left abandoned in the dirt,
such sad reminders of my former life.
When no one’s looking I pick up a few
to save—another painful memory.

And so we live among them, moving camp
with them but keeping to ourselves for fear
they'll take us as their squaws. One thing we do,
we always laugh and say that it is nice,
no matter what it is: watching them dance
or kill, or wading a creek up to our waist
or walking barefoot on the burnt grassland,
we say it's nice, we laugh and say again
how much we are enjoying it, or else....

We learn our friends are drawing near, too close
for comfort for the noble red man—
that's what they're called by poets who don't know
the facts. I never saw nobility
in them, but facts, I think, will show that they
have not been treated well. No one can see
that all are not alike, there's good and bad
(there are good Indians) but no one seems
to notice or to care. They're better off
without the saviours of their souls, I mean,
the noble missionaries. They do more
injury than good, competing with
each other as they do. The Gospel should
be simple, sweet and true, if it's to heal.

I hear the sound of cannon like sweet music
to my ears. I think that liberty
is close—not yet. They say that they have killed
some twenty of the troops while they lost none,
not true. Two men were killed and one the man
who killed my love.

They keep us running with
the squaws, and dig us pits to hide in, wet
and cold and packed. If only I could run!
I hope the troops will follow but in vain.
The next day they have left and my heart sinks.
But for my friend, Mrs. Delaney, I
could easily give way and die. Alas!

A few days after that the fighting braves
collected round our tent to dance and sing
and I fear that the end is very near.
It seems the threat they'd made is likely to
come true, when suddenly they run and scream
and scatter like wild leaves before the wind.
I hang upon Mrs. Delaney's neck
and pray. They ran because they thought they heard
a shot and that's what saved our lives.

    No time
to sigh, we're on the move again from dawn
till dark in heavy rain, so tired when
we stop I cannot sleep. In deep despair
I have no wish to see another day.
There is no certainty for me but death.

May the 31st dawns dark and dim,
turns out to be the best since our lives stopped.
I wake up hearing Pritchard plot escape.
The braves report the troops are still around
and so they plan to move and leave the rest
to follow on.

    This is our chance to flee
—the other way—and so we leave the camp.
For three long days and nights we run, quite lost,
not knowing where we are, but partly free,
still working for these ones they call Métis.
The Pritchards need our help as much as we
need theirs—and so it is this final morn.
Mrs. Delaney bakes the bannock while
I sew for all the Pritchard half-breed kids,
and Mrs. Pritchard says with unfeigned hate,
"They're comin back, les maudits policemen."
I throw the sewing down, the bannock burns
and Mrs. D and I rush out to meet
the scouts just as they gallop into camp.

Rescued! at last, and from a life far worse

than death itself. I'm so relieved I weep
for joy, yet tempered still by loss and pain.
Two of my husband's friends head up the troop
that rescued us. We're glad and say our thanks.

I cannot think I'm safe until we reach
Fort Pitt, and then I do believe it's true.
The men come out to welcome us—alive—
unable to believe that we survived,
they heard such stories of our dreadful fate.
A steamer takes us down to Battleford
and all along the river we see squaws,
men too, run to the banks and wave white flags.
They've washed the war paint off and they
desire rest, perhaps not peace, not yet,
but rest....And so I am retracing steps.

It seems so strange to take a route I took
a few short months ago so different now.
I was a happy bride in love and full
of hope, delighted with the trip, to me
a huge adventure. Life was free to grab.
By contrast now my head is bowed with grief,
I am alone. I'm on my way to friends
but even so I cannot smile. I must
control myself and with God's help I will.
Goodness and mercy surely will be mine,
and if it's not forever I don't care.

It's just as well for us that we don't know
the fate that lies in wait for if we did
we'd never have to courage to get up.
Blind ignorance is bliss, the poet says,
and I would have it so. I never meant
to be a heroine, no never that.
I wanted only to survive. I did.

HANNAH SENESH (1921-1944)
Hungarian Jew, active in the Zionist movement in Palestine. She was killed by the Nazis on a rescue mission in Hungary.

Is there any choice
 between sparkling stars
 and small lights

between yearning
 and longing?

A hard one.

Who said you had a choice?

Life doesn't lead
it drags.

You're on a leash
 back bent knees stiff
 heels dug in sliding...

  Give in!

Not graceful at all
 no grace

Some balm

MISSIE VASSILTCHIKOV (1917-1978)

White Russian aristocrat, caught in Berlin in WWII, Vassiltchikov did office work and kept a diary, permitted by her aristocratic German employers as they plotted to overthrow the Nazi régime.

What I remember best are bombs
and champagne, bubbles of fear,
adrenalin bursting in blood,
sheer animal spirits slake
thirst for life in midst of death.

Trapped in Berlin at beginning of war
with no country and Lithuanian passport,
where to go, what to do?

A job—
make-believe job in make-believe world,
kept because they know, yes, I remember,
they know what I am doing,
my boss Adam and the others, they know
I write diary.

So it will be—they will be remembered.
It will be record of their scheming honour
to kill Hitler.

So little food after bombs begin,
everything rationed, except hats.
I wear hats for cheer,
pretty young woman in frivolous hat, hungry,
ready for party, always champagne.
(My friends' families have wine cellars.)

Slip into shelters at siren's scream,
no one knows where if bomb hits.
Way home lit by fires, home by miracle,
I by miracle, many miracles,
many times spared, intoxicated
drunk with fear.
They talk, I listen,

I take notes, they know.
Writing is on wall, I am fly on wall,
walled in by war.

Long time plotting, short time failing,
backs against wall, they die
traitors. What did they betray?

Not their country, they loved their country.
Not Nazi but German, they died
with their country.

They let me keep job and scribble truth.

THE STEEP OF AGE

MARTHA BALLARD (1735-1812)

Martha Ballard was a New England midwife whose account book became her personal diary.

Great & marvellous are thy sparing mercies O God

Weather clear.
Extracting children adds up year on year.
Sometimes they tarry sometimes me
but safe delivered—so may we all be.

Man works from sun to sun
woman's work is never done
pertickly babies, they keep
coming. I lose sleep
am some fatagud and not much rest.
My house up in arms but I am blest.
Trust God for strength according to my Day.
Yes, give me strength and may
I Conduct accordingly.
Cloudy.

If a child die what to do?
How oft our Expectations die too.
Life like a candle goes out.
Others die too and without
a struggle, hardly pain—
our loss their gain—
leave this world for heaven above
to sing with saints Redeeming love.
This is a world of trial
life but lent to us awhile.

May God teach me to take
the bitter with the sweet and make
me learn my duty.
For the beauty
of the earth may He be praised
and none be raised
above him. I do feel

fatagued but try to conceal
it hold it still
obeying heavenly Parent's will.

The most shocking scene
that was ever seen—
may God grant we take
notice of this and make
a lesson of it, the fate
of a woman murdered by her mate,
and the family, except one son
who fled before the deed was done,
but wounded with an ax.
Such grim facts—
horrid bloodshed,
six children dead.
Life is gone too soon.
Cloudy, rained afternoon.

May it please God to sanctify
this affliction and modify
our hearts. Attended the solemn
funeral and I felt from the bottom
of my heart the pain of all.
(He was interred outside the wall.)

I feel feeble as I go
husband grouses also—
a feeble couple. I'm still needed
and still go unimpeded
where I'm called to babies in the night.

Soon it comes, my long goodnight.
I have been ill, I can no longer care.
The parson came and made a prayer.
I have felt so feeble I am old.
It snowed today, was very cold.

DEBORAH NORRIS LOGAN (1761-1839)

A Philadelphia-born Quaker, Logan began to keep a diary when she was 54, six years before her husband's death. Her diary became her chief companion, an addictive comfort.

Passing down the steep of age
I keep my diary, my friend,
scrawling with scratchy nib
on a clean white sheet
legibly, neat as I was taught,
no eyes but mine to see.

One son died at thirteen, too soon.
One grown son who lived with me
banning pens, needles, books
to save my eyes, shut his, too soon.
My third son has sent his son
to help me down the slope.
He doesn't talk.

I do not have a pen to write with.
If God would grant me a decent pen
I'll keep on writing folly.
No one can see.

If I don't do it
nothing is done right.
Without reproof my maids all leave
only cook stays.
Sometimes I am alone for days
but for my birds, a dog, and Puss—
all the same with different names—
They stay with me.

I would nestle my grandchild
as a dove in my bosom.
She is my cordial
in the cup of life.

Dear Reader, thee will be kind,

I did not have thee in mind.
I am not foolish but old
and sometimes alone,
no creature but Puss
to keep me company.

I am doomed to wretched pens.

Weaned from life, I see the world
falling away. I wish...
wielding a hateful pen I wish
to write
something new.

I want comfort.
It is essential to my comfort
to have black ink
and good pens.
Evil instruments
spoil the page.
I age, I age.

BIBLIOGRAPHY

Alcott, Louisa May
The Journals of Louisa May Alcott, ed. Joel Myerson & Daniel Shealy; associate ed. Madelein B. Stern, Little, Brown & Company, Boston, Toronto, London, 1989

Bauman, Janina
Winter in the Morning: A Young Girl's Life in the Warsaw Ghetto and Beyond, 1939-1945, The Free Press, New York, 1986

Bird, Isabella L.
A Lady's Life in the Rocky Mountains (1873), University of Oklahoma Press, Norman and London, 1988

Blodgett, Harriet
Source of material for Hester Thrale Piozzi and Lady Margaret Hoby, diary excerpts in:Centuries of Female Days: Englishwomen's Private Diaries, Rutgers University Press, New Brunswick, N.J., 1988—, The Englishwoman's Diary: An Anthology ed. Blodgett,Fourth Estate, London, 1991, (c) by the Rector and visitors of the University of Virginia

Burney, Fanny
Fanny Burney: Selected Letters and Journals , ed. Joyce Hemlow, Oxford University Press, New York, 1987

Chesnut, Mary Boykin
The Private Mary Chesnut: The Unpublished Civil War Diaries, ed. C. Vann Woodward, Elizabeth Muhlenfeld, Oxford University Press, New York, Oxford, 1984

Cullwick, Hannah
The Diaries of Hannah Cullwick, Victorian Maidservant , ed. Liz Stanley. Rutgers University Press, New Brunswick, N.J., 1984

Dessaulles, Henriette
Hopes and Dreams: The Diary of Henriette Dessaulles, 1874-1881, tr. Liedewy Hawke Hounslow Press, Willowdale, Ontario, 1971

Durham, Lady Louisa Lambton
Letters & Diaries of Lady Durham , ed. Patricia Godsell Oberon Press, Canada, 1979

Ellice, Jane
The Diary of Jane Ellice, ed. Patricia Godsell, Oberon Press, Canada, 1975

Franklin, Penelope
Private Pages: Diaries of American Women, 1830s-1970s, Ballantine Books, New York, 1986, (source of material for Deborah Norris Logan)

Holliday, Laurel, ed.
Heart Songs: The Intimate Diaries of Young Girls, Guerneville, California: Bluestocking Books, 1978 (includes excerpts from an early diary of Kathie Gray (pseudonym) 1864-??)

Langton, Anne
A Gentlewoman in Upper Canada: The Journals of Anne Langton, ed. H.H. Langton, Irwin Publishing, Toronto, 1950

Lensink, Judy Nolte, ed.
"A Secret to be Burried" The Diary and Life of Emily Hawley Gillespie, 1858-1888 , University of Iowa Press, Iowa City, 1989

Lord, Margaret Gray
One Woman's Charlottetown: Diaries of Margaret Gray Lord, 1863, 1876, 1890, ed. Evelyn J. MacLeod, Canadian Museum of Civilization, National Museums of Canada, 1988

MacLane, Mary
The Story of Mary MacLane, by Herself, Chicago: Herbert S. Stone, 1902
I, Mary MacLane: A Diary of Human Days, Frederick A. Stokes Co., New York, 1917, (both books out of print, but there's a copy of each in the Schlesinger Library, Radcliffe College, Cambridge, MA)

McGowan, Nellie
The Diary of Nellie McGowan, Partridge Island Quarantine Station, 1902. Harold E. Wright, ed., St. John: Partridge Island Research Project, 1984.

Mead, Margaret
An Anthropologist at Work: Writings of Ruth Benedict, (containing excerpts from Benedict's diaries),Houghton Mifflin, Boston, 1959

Modersohn-Becker, Paula
Paula Modersohn-Becker: The Letters and Journals, ed. Gunter Busch and Liselotte von Reinken; ed. and tr. Arthur S. Wensinger and Carole Clew HoeyTaplinger Publishing, New York, 1983

Scott, Evelyn
Escapade: An Autobiography, Carroll & Graf Publishers, New York, 1987 (first published 1923)_Senesh, Hannah. Hannah Senesh: Her Life and Diary Schocken Books, New York, 1973

Shonagon, Sei,
The Pillow Book of Sei Shonagon, tr. and ed. Ivan Morris, Penguin Books, London, 1967

Tolstoy, Sophia
The Diaries of Sophia Tolstoy, tr. Cathy Porter, New York: Random House, 1985

Ulrich, Laurel Thatcher
A Midwife's Tale: The Life of Martha Ballard,
Based on Her Diary, Alfred A. Knopf, New York, 1990

Vassiltchikov, Marie ("Missie")
The Berlin Diaries, 1940-1945, The Folio Society, London, 1991

Wordsworth, Dorothy
The Grasmere Journal , Henry Holt & Company, New York, 1987

Zaremba, Eve
ed. Privilege of Sex, A Century of Canadian Women, Anansi, Toronto, 1974, (includes Theresa Gowanlock's account of "Two Months in the Camp of Big Bear")